MOMENTS WITH ONESELF

ACTION AND REACTION

SWAMI DAYANANDA SARASWATI
Arsha Vidya

Arsha Vidya Research
and Publication Trust
Chennai

Published by :

Arsha Vidya Research and Publication Trust
4 ' Sri Nidhi ' Apts 3rd Floor
Sir Desika Road Mylapore
Chennai 600 004 INDIA
Tel : 044 2499 7023
Telefax : 2499 7131
Email : avrandpt@gmail.com
Website: www.avrpt.com

ISBN : 978 - 81 - 904203 - 4 - 1

Revised Edition	: April	2007	Copies	: 1500
1st Reprint	: May	2009	Copies	: 2000
2nd Reprint	: March	2011	Copies	: 1000
3rd Reprint	: May	2012	Copies	: 1000
4th Reprint	: October	2013	Copies	: 1000

Design & Layout:
Graaphic Design

Printed at :
Sudarsan Graphics
27, Neelakanta Mehta Street
T. Nagar, Chennai 600 017
Email : info@sudarsan.com

Contents

Key to Transliteration and Pronunciation of Sanskrit Letters

Sanskrit is a highly phonetic language and hence accuracy in articulation of the letters is important. For those unfamiliar with the *Devanāgari* script, the international transliteration is a guide to the proper pronunciation of Sanskrit letters.

अ	*a*	*(but)*	ट	*ṭa*	*(true)**3
आ	*ā*	*(father)*	ठ	*ṭha*	*(anthill)**3
इ	*i*	*(it)*	ड	*ḍa*	*(drum)**3
ई	*ī*	*(beat)*	ढ	*ḍha*	*(godhead)**3
उ	*u*	*(full)*	ण	*ṇa*	*(under)**3
ऊ	*ū*	*(pool)*	त	*ta*	*(path)**4
ऋ	*ṛ*	*(rhythm)*	थ	*tha*	*(thunder)**4
ॠ	*ṝ*	*(marine)*	द	*da*	*(that)**4
ऌ	*ḷ*	*(revelry)*	ध	*dha*	*(breathe)**4
ए	*e*	*(play)*	न	*na*	*(nut)**4
ऐ	*ai*	*(aisle)*	प	*pa*	*(put)* 5
ओ	*o*	*(go)*	फ	*pha*	*(loophole)**5
औ	*au*	*(loud)*	ब	*ba*	*(bin)* 5
क	*ka*	*(seek)* 1	भ	*bha*	*(abhor)**5
ख	*kha*	*(blockhead)**1	म	*ma*	*(much)* 5
ग	*ga*	*(get)* 1	य	*ya*	*(loyal)*
घ	*gha*	*(log hut)**1	र	*ra*	*(red)*
ङ	*ṅa*	*(sing)* 1	ल	*la*	*(luck)*
च	*ca*	*(chunk)* 2	व	*va*	*(vase)*
छ	*cha*	*(catch him)**2	श	*śa*	*(sure)*
ज	*ja*	*(jump)* 2	ष	*ṣa*	*(shun)*
झ	*jha*	*(hedgehog)**2	स	*sa*	*(so)*
ञ	*ña*	*(bunch)* 2	ह	*ha*	*(hum)*

ं	ṁ	*anusvāra*	(nasalisation of preceding vowel)
:	ḥ	*visarga*	(aspiration of preceding vowel)
*			No exact English equivalents for these letters

1.	Guttural	–	Pronounced from throat
2.	Palatal	–	Pronounced from palate
3.	Lingual	–	Pronounced from cerebrum
4.	Dental	–	Pronounced from teeth
5.	Labial	–	Pronounced from lips

The 5th letter of each of the above class – called nasals – are also pronounced nasally.

LIFE IS ROLE PLAYING

Action and reaction, as we know from physics, are both equal and opposite. You cannot rub against something without yourself getting rubbed in the process. However, I am looking at these two words with reference to your response to the world.

LIFE INVOLVES RELATIONSHIP

You cannot avoid relating as well as responding to the world, whether you like it.[1] You must necessarily relate to the world in order to live your life; you need not relate to the world just to be alive. When you are in deep sleep, you are alive but you do not relate to the world; there is no world, in fact, for you. There is no relationship, no memories, no situational problems to cause any concern. You are just alive; you merely exist. You can exist even in a state of coma, without relating to the world. It is possible to keep a person alive in coma for years on life support systems. However, that is not living. To live your life, you need to relate to the world.

---

[1] Whether or not is a common expression but the correct usage is only 'whether' without being followed by 'or not'. Whether one likes this, grammatically this is right (Author).

Any relationship implies two factors: one is you, the person who relates, and the other is what or whom you relate to. Of these two, one is a changing factor, that which you are related to. The situation to which you are related keeps on changing all the time and the change can be total. Now you see fire and now you see a stream of water; two things entirely different in nature. You meet your father and the next moment you meet your son. The object has completely changed, the son replacing the father. In terms of sensory perceptions, form, smell, sound, touch or taste, the objects you perceive constantly change. Thus, the world you confront keeps changing whereas you, the one who confronts the world, is invariable. A person who sees a form is the same who hears a sound. The one who saw and heard is the one who is talking to someone now. So, the person, 'you' remains the same, whereas the objects keep changing. Therefore, we can say that, of the two factors involved in relating, one is variable and the other, the one who confronts, is invariable. You are the same person whether you relate to father or son, uncle or husband, friends or foe, employer or employee. You are the same whether you see or hear, walk or talk, sing or smell. This is true even from the standpoint of mental activities: the one who doubts is the one who decides; the one who loves is the one who hates; the one who is kind is the one who is cruel. The person is invariable and that is you.

THE INVARIABLE FACTOR

We need to look into the 'you' that is invariable. Is it totally invariable? We cannot say so because there seems to be a variable status even for the subject, the person who relates, in keeping with what or whom he or she relates. When you relate to your father either mentally or perceptually, you are a son. Again, when you relate to your son, you are no longer the previous person, the son; you are now a father. You undergo a change. The subject 'I' that was a son while relating to the father has changed to become a father while relating to the son. The person 'I' is there but he or she has a different status now. To a sister, the 'I' is a brother; to a wife, the 'I' is a husband; to a student the 'I' is a teacher and to a teacher the 'I' is a student. Thus, because of a relationship, the 'I' also undergoes change.

The change in the 'I' is not total as is the case with the objects with which the 'I' relates. The object can be a form perceived earlier which is totally replaced by a sound heard now. The object can be a friend that is totally replaced by another, a stranger, the exact opposite.

There is something that I like and something that I do not like. Thus the change in the object is total though the subject 'I' is not totally replaced. If it is, there will be no continuity at all. The father-I is replaced by the son-I, but the 'I' is not totally replaced. If it is totally replaced, there will be neither father nor son because the one who related to the son has vanished, while a new one who has appeared in his place cannot have a relationship with the father. If an invariable factor is not there in the subject, there will be no thread to connect the experiences. Hence, the subject does undergo a change in relation to the object but the change is not total; it is incidental and partial.

The partial change in the subject 'I' does not seem to leave any trace upon the 'I'. Imagine that while you are talking to your sister, your wife comes along and you start talking to her. In relation to your wife, the brother goes away completely and the husband has taken his place. You are very much there, remember, because the one who was a brother is the same who is now the husband. At the same time, the previous role does not leave a trace upon you, the subject. Therefore, you are able to assume a new role altogether without suffering a change on your part. It reveals a great fact about life. It is an amazing capacity to undergo change when you relate to something without intrinsically undergoing change. It is this capacity that makes your life imbued with freshness and freedom. If you do not recognise this fact fully, it is indeed a great tragedy and life becomes a misery.

The invariable factor 'I' undergoes a seeming change with reference to a particular situation. When you come in contact with an object that you like you become a liker. The next moment, if you come in contact with an object that you dislike, you immediately become a disliker. In both these situations the 'I' is very much present. This 'I' is invariable and is, therefore, neither a liker nor a disliker. Is it not true? If you know this to be true, you have made your life.

If there is the presence of the 'I' in all situations undergoing seeming changes, we can look at the situation as we would look at an actor who assumes different roles. Let us assume that in a play there is an actor A taking on the role of a beggar B who also happens to be the hero of the play. Naturally, he is paid a lot of money for the role of a beggar because he plays the role very well, having studied the mannerisms and modes of begging of many beggars in the streets. In addition, he has music in the background to emphasise the emotions of a beggar, which a real life beggar on the street does not have. Actor A is therefore a very effective beggar on stage. People insult him, spit on him, but he takes it all in his stride without any protest. Some give him alms, which he accepts with a smile. Sometimes he sheds tears and he is such a great actor that he is able to bring real tears almost at will. He undergoes various experiences, pleasant and painful, joyful and tragic. Please tell me if these experiences affect the actor A? Is he affected by the problems belonging to the role B? No. Even while shedding tears, he is aware that he is playing a rọle. Within himself, however, he is happy because he is acting the part so well. This is possible because he did not lose himself to the role; he is self-aware.

Let us suppose, instead, that the actor gets carried away by the role, thinking that he is a real beggar, then he is no longer acting; he is reacting. If there should be a villain in the play and there is an encounter between the two characters, the villain is expected to hit the beggar who has to receive without retaliation. However, the beggar forgets his role, hits back and punches the villain.

He was not expected to punish the villain; it was not according to the script. The curtain comes down and the play is stopped in the middle. When the director asks the actor to explain, the beggar says, "I hit him because he hit me. How can he hit me?" His hitting back is a reaction; something happened within him. At that moment, he forgot that he was an actor playing a role. Normally, the problems of the role are confined to the role. They do not affect the actor. Mr A, the actor, does not subject himself to the problems of B. It means there is a distance between B and A, which is why the problems of B do not affect A. Is there a physical distance between these two? No. B's nose is A's nose; B's eyes are A's eyes; B's body is A's body and B's mind is A's mind. B does not have an independent status. He does not have a being of his own. B does not enjoy an 'I' for himself. B does not have an *ātman* for himself. Therefore B is A. Does it mean that B's problems are A's? This can be true only if B is A and A is B. The problems of one would become the problems of the other. However, here the role B is A, but A is not B.

The fact that A is not B comes into play not only when the role B is cast off, but that A is not B even while playing the role B. You must understand this clearly. This is called *jñāna*, knowledge. Actor A need not give up the role B in order to be A; that happens in deep sleep and coma, but not in real life. Life is characterised by relationships. If A is not B, why should it be necessary to give up B in order to own up A? In fact, A should be able to go from B to C, from C to D and so on; yet A remains A.

You can understand clearly that while B is A, A is not B. A is not affected by the problems of B because A is aware of the fact that he is A playing the role B. He does not lose self-awareness even while being totally identified with the role. When A plays the role retaining his self-identity clearly, there is only action, not reaction.

ROLES CANNOT BE AVOIDED

While the role B depends entirely upon the actor A, A does not depend upon B.[2] This is not an ordinary fact. It is a fact that everyone should necessarily know because when you are an actor, you have to be disciplined enough not to be carried away by a role, in a given situation. When the actor cannot handle the role he is given to play, he can be told to give up playing roles. However, is it possible for you and me to avoid roles?

In real life the roles land upon you sometimes even without your knowledge. As you are born, the father says, "A son is born." The brother says, "A brother is born." Others can say, "A grandson is born; a cousin is born," and so on. A demographer will say that, "our population

---

[2] Compare *Bhagavad Gītā* (9.4)
matsthāni sarvabhūtāni na cāhaṁ teṣvavasthitaḥ
All beings depend upon me, but I do not depend upon them.

has increased by one more member." Before you know anything, you are already related. Birth itself is a relationship. You are born related, you live related — it means you have to play roles.

Even while using the senses, you play a role. When you see, you are a seer. However, does the 'I' have the intrinsic attribute of seeing? If so, you should be seeing all the time. The truth, however, is that sometimes you are a seer, hearer thinker, walker, eater and so on. The 'I' remains the same. The 'I' assumes the roles of seer, hearer and so on, but you are none of them. Therefore, Lord Kṛṣṇa says, in the *Bhagavad Gītā*:[3] "In the city of nine gates, he rests happily, neither doing nor making anyone do."

The wise person performs actions without performing them because there is a distance between the role and the player. It is not a physical distance; the distance is knowledge. The wise man knows the true identity of 'I' and is aware of the fact that he is playing roles on stage.

My status, therefore, is very clear. The incidental status that I get is a role and the 'I' is always invariable in all of them. The person who has self-identity

[3] *navadvāre pure dehī naiva kurvanna kārayan* (5.13)

understands that the roles are not intrinsic to the self. Seeing is not possible without 'I' but the 'I' is not merely a seer. It is a fact. If this is so, my entire life becomes one of role-playing. Neither you nor I nor anyone else can avoid playing roles. Since I cannot avoid role-playing, I have no choice in knowing the person who plays the roles. I have neither a choice in playing the roles nor do I have a choice in understanding myself as I am. The reason is that if I do not know the 'I' who plays the roles, then I become the roles. My whole life then becomes a tragedy.

While playing the role of a father, if I am aware of the fact that I am playing a role, then father merely becomes a role. I do not require reminding myself of my identity that I am not the role because the knowledge of the actor is always there in the background. I do not have to deliberately remember myself. Thus, when I play the role of a father in my life, I know I am playing a role according to the script, and to the best of my knowledge and ability. However, no one has all the knowledge and all the ability, which is why sometimes I may do things that are not right, that may not work, but that is acceptable. What is important is that I know I am playing a role, that I do not become the role.

WHEN THE ACTOR BECOMES THE ROLE

Unfortunately, in our upbringing there is no occasion to know the 'I,'the person who plays the roles. Right from birth, we play roles, as son, father, mother, husband and so on. However, there is no occasion when we can really take a look at ourselves deliberately. Shorn of all roles we do not know the 'I' that plays the roles. Yet we are called upon to play roles. When we do not know the person who plays the role, the role becomes the person. Thus, when one plays the role of father without knowing the 'I' the role becomes real; one becomes the father.

Let us look at the father who has a son growing up in his own fashion. The father did the best he could to bring up the son. As long as the son was in school, it looked as though he would fulfil the father's hopes and wishes. The father had hoped that his son would become a scientist. However, as soon as the son went to college, he changed. All that he does now is go around on a motorbike which has no silencer, wearing jeans and shirt unbuttoned. The father is so disappointed that whenever he thinks of his son his blood pressure rises. The reason is that the father thinks that he is father, a real life father. The father in him lingers on even while talking to his wife and at work. He remains an angry father, an angry husband the whole day because he cannot get rid of the son from his mind. The father, the husband is no longer a role. The role and the person have merged; they have become one. However, what we have in reality is a person, not a father or a husband. The man is a husband only in relation to this woman. Similarly, with the woman, she is a wife only in relation to this man.

There is no real wife or husband or son or brother in the world. There are only persons playing different roles in relation to different situations. When this fact is not known, the roles become the person. The problems of the role become the problems of the person. If the role of a father becomes a problem, every other role also becomes a problem. When he or she drives a car, for instance, it becomes a problem because he or she is not aware that the driver is a role; the person becomes a pack of nerves.

ROLES BRING CHALLENGES

Any role that I play becomes a problem because there are no roles or situations without problems. If I have a nose, I will catch cold. I cannot live a life related to situations without challenges, without problems. In fact, life itself is a drama because every role has a number of turning situations. Everything appears to be rosy, very purple and very beautiful when all of a sudden, in one stroke, everything changes. There is thunder and lightning; the clouds burst open and everything is wet with tears. As the situation changes, so do the clouds and tears, giving way to sun and stars. Thus, situations in life change constantly.

No role-playing is going to be smooth sailing. In fact, there is no fun sailing in smooth waters all the time. Sailing is an exciting adventure because there are winds, sometimes favourable and sometimes not. The waves are not always conducive. At such times, when we wish to take our boat in a particular direction, it will be a challenge. It is challenges that make life interesting.

Imagine a movie without plots, without excitement. It would be insipid. Similarly, one cannot imagine playing the role of a father or mother, uncle or cousin, employer or employee without challenges. One cannot imagine being a thinker without a challenging question that requires a solution. One cannot imagine an economic issue without posing challenges. One cannot imagine a driver without a traffic situation. One cannot even imagine being a walker without the possibility of missing a step. This is the fun of role-playing. A drama is a drama only when it has this pattern of plots that change all the time. Therefore, if one has to play the roles, one better learns to be familiar with oneself, with the person who plays the roles, who is free from the roles, and who is untouched by the roles.

THE PERSON AND THE PERSONALITY

PURUṢA AND PRAKṚTI

In Sanskrit, the person is called *puruṣa*.[4] It is the *puruṣa* who plays different roles such as seer, hearer, thinker and so on. The *puruṣa* is endowed with a three-fold faculty called *prakṛti* which consists of the mind, the organs of perception, the vital force, the organs of action, and the physical body. *Puruṣa* and *prakṛti* are not really two different entities. The *prakṛti* does not have an independent status, it is the *puruṣa* who is independent. The *prakṛti* has three-fold powers – *jñāna-śakti*, the power to know including memory; *icchā-śakti*, the power to will including desire, doubt, emotions, and *kriyā-śakti*, the power to act including skill, creative power and so on.

Presiding over the *prakṛti*, the *puruṣa* enjoys this three-fold power. The power to know enables us to gather knowledge to the extent of our capacity. With the power to desire, a great power indeed, we can entertain any number of desires, while the power to act helps us to

---

[4] *puri śayanāt puruṣaḥ*, the one who dwells in the city (body) is called *puruṣaḥ*.

fulfil these desires. Role-playing, such as knower, desirer, and doer, is involved in employing these powers. However, these roles belong to *prakṛti*, while the *puruṣa* remains independent of them. A person has roles to play in life, and so he needs to understand the roles as roles and the person as person. A role becomes a role only when the person is clearly understood. This is called discrimination, *viveka-jñāna*, a knowledge that comes with the study of the *śāstra*. Without this clear understanding of the nature of the *puruṣa*, the roles become real and the person is forgotten. When A becomes B, the *puruṣa* becomes the role and the problems of the role become the problems of the person. With clear understanding, however, we can handle the challenges without being affected. Challenge is a fact while reaction is a problem. If we act upon the challenge, then we are acting on a fact.

Thus, we can identify two kinds of problems: Problems centred on roles or facts, and problems centred on 'I'. For instance, if there is a lack of money, comforts and facilities, I can act upon it to remove the lack. However, if this lack of wealth makes me jealous of someone who has these facilities, it is another kind of problem, a problem centred on 'I'. Such a problem makes me sad and frustrated. At such times, the capacities that

I have, knowledge, action and skill, none of these become available, overpowered as they are by my jealousy and so on. My reactions deny me the very power I have in command to meet the challenging situations. When I react, I have denied myself the powers I have that may be adequate to meet the situation successfully.

REACTION IS A HAPPENING

A reaction is a happening; it is not a conscious decision. It does not consult your knowledge, status, culture, age, anything. You may have accomplished all these so far in your life, but when they are not consulted while responding to a situation, they are as good as not being there. Anger, for instance, is a reaction. Try as you may, you cannot become angry consciously. You can, at best, pretend to be angry; you can raise your voice, look stern and so on, but you are not an angry person. Even your son can make out that you are pretending to be angry. If you are really angry, your son will be nowhere around. The difference is obvious even to a child. It is one thing to be strict or stern deliberately, since you know what you are doing and the reason for doing it. However, it is quite another to be really angry because you will not be aware of what you are doing in anger. It is like the story of the *guru* and his disciple. The *guru* wanted to rest and asked his disciple to watch out for flies and insects. As it usually happens, a fly kept buzzing around the *guru*'s nose, despite the disciple's all efforts to chase it away. The disciple became so angry that he took a big stone and hit the fly while it was on the *guru*'s nose. The fly died, but the *guru* also never woke up!

So, when a reaction such as anger comes, all your reasoning disappears. Your wisdom is relegated to the background and the one who responds is altogether a different person, a person controlled by anger or whatever emotion that has arisen. Further, it is not possible for you to be consciously angry or jealous or frustrated or agitated or sad, no matter how hard you try. You can understand clearly, that reactions are mechanical. If you can make sure that these reactions do not occur, then you will be able to respond to situations. You will have no problem in handling the situations. The problem, however, is that you are not able to manage your reactions and your resolve not to react is invariably broken.

ROLE-PLAYING IS KARMA-YOGA

To know that the *puruṣa* merely plays a role and is not the role is itself a great relief. When I understand that I am not a real life husband and that I only play the role of a husband, it relieves me of the problem of the role. Further, once I know that husband is a role, wife is a role, mother is a role, all I have to do is to play the role according to the script. When the *Bhagavad Gītā* talks of *svakarma*, it is referring to actions according to the script. Every role has a script and if I can consciously follow the script, my life becomes one of *karma-yoga*.

Role-playing is one way of participating in the creation. In the vision of the Veda, the Lord is both the creator and the creation. He is both the intelligent as well as the material cause of the creation. After creating everything Lord does not go to sleep. He remains active, dynamic, as is evident from the creation itself. Īśvara, the Lord, in his role as creator is called Brahmā; in his role as protector or sustainer he is Viṣṇu; in the role of destroyer he is Rudra. He is constantly playing all these roles. Every moment there is creation in the sense there is birth of new things. Equally every moment there is sustenance as well as destruction as there are old things being destroyed to give way to new. This cyclic process sustained in a meaningful way provides harmony of the creation. If we look at time for instance, a moment is born, it is and it is gone. What is the time involved in this? What is the distance between birth and sustenance?

Between sustenance and death? The three aspects of Īśvara function simultaneously, as he plays his roles effortlessly.

In the creation, therefore, I am the person who is born in the world with an individual body, mind, senses and organs of action. Since I am endowed with all these, I am not meant to be a mere passive observer of the world. Why was I endowed with limbs and senses? If I were meant to be a mere observer, I would have only a head without other limbs. But, this is not the case. I am endowed with the power to know, to will and act. Further, the necessary resources are provided in the creation to employ these powers. Therefore, I am meant to be an active participant in the scheme of things. Participation means playing roles. *Puruṣa* only plays the roles without any involvement; it is the *prakṛti* who is involved in role-playing. The *puruṣa* becomes the basis of the roles that are played, hence remains intrinsically untouched. The roles leave no trace upon him.

Playing the roles according to the given script is what is called as *karma-yoga*. You know the scripts or you learn of them from the scripture or from those who know. There are no problems when you play roles. There is a choice in certain roles. Hence, if you find a given role difficult, you can choose not to play it or you can choose another according to your preference. You have to take care, of course, that your choice of roles does not affect your other roles. In life, more often than not, there are no choices. You are born a son to your parents; you have no choice. Your son is born to you and you become his father; now again you have no choice to be a father. So there are many roles you have to play over which you have no choice or limited choice. Actually, the so-called difficult roles bring out your strength, your talent. The problem does not lie in the role; the problem lies in your thinking that you are the role. Being a husband or a wife is not a problem but mistaking the person as the very role is the problem.

REACTIONS CREATE PERSONALITY

If I tell you, "Do not react," it is not going to work because, as I said earlier, a reaction is a happening that does not consult you. You may react to this very advice. A person came to see me and said that he no longer gets angry.

"Swamiji, I do not get angry these days."

"No, I do not think so."

"No, Swamiji. I really do not get angry these days."

"I do not think that is true. I think you will get angry when the required situation arises."

"No, Swamiji. I do not get angry."

"I am sure you will get angry."

You can imagine how he responded to my persistent stand. He raised his voice and said, "Don't you hear what I say? I do not get angry."

I said quickly, "Yes, yes, you are right."

I stopped because I did not want him to get angry. He was very controlled up to a point. After that, he showed signs of breaking down. It is obvious that a mere resolve is not enough because a reaction is a happening. It does not consult you. It is, therefore, unpredictable.

The reason is that each person is a personality. The *puruṣa* is a simple being, pure, beautiful, and full. It is the personality that each one is that creates problems. Personality is nothing but a collection of in-built reactions.

While playing different roles, you gather a number of reactions that you are not permitted to express. Let us look at a situation in an office. You have a boss who feels free to say what he wishes and free to do what he wants. He asks you to pass an order. You do not think that it is proper but you do not know how to say 'no' to your boss. He may feel slighted because he has his own psychological problems. He is vulnerable to any suggestion that amounts to mean he is wrong. This is his weak point, if you press it hard enough, he is bound to react. There are times of course when you do tell him because you are a person who cannot act upon something that you know is wrong. At such times, the boss gets angry and calls you names. You are equally angry because you have your own problems and weak points. The boss, however, is in a position to vent his anger while you are not. You have to swallow your anger because you do not want to lose your job, losing the job will cause you a lot of problems at home. For the sake of peace at home, you swallow your anger, but the anger, where will it go? It cannot go anywhere. It remains fuming within you and forms part of the bedrock of your personality.

If the role of an employee is difficult, no less difficult is the role of a father, daughter, mother and so on. Every role-playing appears to be fraught with problems. It is not that role-playing has become more difficult, but that one has less insight about oneself. You need to move from role to role, but if each role leaves its mark then even roles get influenced by roles.

Here is a man who has had a quarrel with his wife. He comes out of the house and shuts the door with a bang. The way he shut the door reveals that the husband is still there. Even though he has left his wife, there is a hangover of the husband. It happens because the husband was not just a role; it has rolled into the person. His anger continues and reveals itself when he opens the door of his car, the way he starts the engine, the way he drives and arrives at the office. The husband is still there! This is how one role overlaps the other, resulting in a build-up of reactions crystallising into a personality.

So we find everyone is a personality made up of leftover reactions such as anger, jealousy, hatred, frustration and so on. Everyone, therefore, is vulnerable. There are buttons inside the personality and the moment the button is touched, the person blows up. The wife knows the areas where her husband will get angry. She even cautions the children to keep away from asking certain things or creating certain situations.

Thus, everyone is a personality, predictable and unpredictable; they are no longer persons. Such persons make a home dysfunctional.

THE PERSON IS FREE

KNOW THE PERSON FREE FROM PERSONALITY

To know the person, you have to understand that reactions stem from person-role confusion. You can resolve the confusion by being familiar with the *puruṣa*, the self, the non-responding bare self that does not brand things as good or bad. Whenever you see nature such as the blue sky, the stars, the birds, the flowers, you remark, "Oh, how beautiful." At that time, you are happy, a pleased person. When you are busy, your mind is occupied or restless. You are unable to appreciate beauty. You do not have the inner leisure to appreciate beauty. When you appreciate beauty and say, "Oh, how beautiful this is," you see the beauty in 'this'. However, with further understanding, you realise that the beauty you appreciate is yourself, the pleased self. It is a pleasure when you find beauty in an object, but it becomes a meditation when you understand that it is the beauty of the self that you appreciate. It is you; the pleased self is you. If you see this during every enjoyable experience, every such experience becomes yoga, self-appreciation.

There are situations that bring out of you this silent appreciative person. The personality with hundreds of likes and dislikes and demands, that normally comes out to respond to the world, is silenced by certain overwhelming situations, the situations that are at once profound, striking and pleasing. A person, an event, a scene, even a joke, can bring out of you this appreciative person. When you see yourself in that happiness or enjoyment or silence, there is self-appreciation, self-recognition, and self-acceptance. You now have a chance, an opportunity, to be familiar with yourself. It is the way to get rid of reactions because it becomes clear that reactions do not belong to the person. They are born of the person-role confusion. When such discrimination is there, reactions lose their support system; they are orphaned.

PERSONALITY IS FALSE

One good thing about reactions is that they are false. You need to understand that the person is real because he or she is always the same, ever present, silent, complete being. The personality is false because it is subject to being dismissed. In deep sleep or in moments of joy, the personality disappears, but the person remains. The person is very much there even when the personality is reacting to situations. It is the role that depends on you; you are independent of the role. The role, therefore, is neither real nor unreal. It is *mithyā*. The actions born of this *mithyā* are not different; they are also *mithyā*. Both actions and reactions do not impact the person. If they do affect the person, it is because of confusion about the person and the role. You have not looked into the nature of the person. It is like an ill-kept house, neglected for a long time. However, once you look into the self in order to understand, your whole life becomes meditation.

Once you recognise that reactions are false, you will be resolved of the person-role confusion. They may have left deep impressions in your mind, but even these impressions are false. They do not and cannot impinge upon the 'I'. If they affect the 'I' you cannot appreciate anything. When you appreciate a flower or look at the sky as it is, where are these impressions or *saṁskāra*s or *vāsanā*s?

The self always remains the same, untouched by the reactions or impressions. It has never gathered anything at any time. Bondage, impurity, *rāga*, *dveṣa* or *vāsanā*s, none of these are in the self. All that you have is a mind with some memories. The whole problem is nothing but built-up reactions, which belong to the roles. Hence, they are only true as roles and nothing more. A wave does not have a reality of its own; it has its being in water. Water is *satya,* real and wave is *mithyā,* false. Wave is a role that water takes. The birth and death of a wave or its size are as true as the wave; they are *mithyā*. What matters is water. Water remains the same, regardless of waves, which leave no impressions upon the water. Similarly, the roles leave no impression on the self. I have to play roles, you have to play roles and everyone has to play roles; you better become familiar with the self as a person free from roles. This is meditation.

MEDITATION IS AN APPOINTMENT WITH THE SELF

The meditation that I am talking about is the meditation said by Lord Kṛṣṇa in the *Bhagavad Gītā*:[5] "Bring the mind to yourself and do not think of anything else."

In meditation, it is important to know who meditates. There are varieties of meditation prevalent these days. Some want you to look at the tip of the nose, some between the eyebrows, some a point within and so on. But who is the one who meditates? If the meditator is

---

[5] *ātmasaṁsthaṁ manaḥ kṛtvā na kiñcidapi cintayet* (6.25)

taken care of, the meditation will take care of itself. I would say, meditation is an appointment with yourself, nothing more. You may say that it is an appointment with the Lord which amounts to an appointment with yourself; there is no difference. If it is an appointment with yourself, you need to be free from roles. You must be A, while the person and the roles, B, C, D and so on, are different from you. Normally, you take yourself to be the roles, overlooking or unaware of the person A. Therefore, meditation is just in keeping with the teaching. You should know what A is, without being B, C or D, even while playing the roles of B, C or D.

You generally react in the roles. Therefore, all the roles are embedded in the personality that has become a reactor, a fuming reactor. The reactions overpower the person. If you can learn to be yourself, shedding all the roles, then that meditation is the supreme action. You are aware of yourself as a person. It is a very important fact because you give up the embedded father, embedded daughter, embedded wife, embedded mother and so on. Then, the three powers, the power to know, to desire and to act, are at your command. Meditation, as a programme, is therefore very necessary.

Meditation

You sit in a relaxed posture.
Close your eyes and just be yourself

Be yourself, free from roles
Visualise the blue sky...
Mountains, trees, streams ...

Do you want the sky to be different in any way?

No

When you appreciate
The blue sky
You are a non-demanding person

Look at yourself

How appreciative you are
Pleased with the self
That is the person you are
Aware and conscious

Think of the stars...

Let the sky be studded with stars...

Again look at yourself

Think of mountains...

A body of clouds...

The rising sun...

The setting sun...

The ocean...

Visualise trees...

Flowers

Fully blossomed flowers
On the bushes...

Look at the birds

The free ones flying in the sky...

Just visualise them, mentally

Now, look at yourself
How are you?

You are a simple...

Pleased...

Awareful person...

You are yourself
Non-demanding...

Without likes or dislikes.

Being yourself
You are familiar with
That non-demanding person

Now, visualise situations
That generally bring out reactions in you...

When you visualised the stars, sky, trees
They did not cause
Any reaction in you...

Now, visualise situations
To which you normally react...

Suppose there is a person
Who has hurt you deeply...

Or you think that destiny
Has robbed you of something...
Or deprived you of something...
Or death has taken away
Somebody from you...

Look at those situations
To which you reacted...
With sadness, anger and so on...

Meditation is to look at these situations
With the same person

Who related to the sky...

Who appreciated the stars...

The sky...

The mountains...

The rivers...

The non-demanding

Appreciative person

Try to bring that person

To bear upon these situations

That normally bring about reactions

In you

Look at the situations
no matter how serious or grave
They may be

If a situation requires
A response from you...

If the situation needs a change...

Do whatever has to be done

Bring about the change

If it makes the situation

Easy or more comfortable for you

It does not require a reaction

It requires action

In meditation

You look at yourself

In a situation

That you desire...

You wish

For something to happen...

You look at yourself

In a situation

That you dislike...

You wish to be rid of...

With reference to any of these situations

You see yourself the pleased...

The non-demanding person

All those residual, embedded reactions

Disappear

Because they are false

The reactions have no status of their own
If you have some desires...

Let them be

If there is the subconscious...

The unconscious...

Let them be

You are just the simple person
Who is free...

Intrinsically free from any affliction

This is you

You do not need

To do anything to be you

Fire does not do

Anything to be hot

You do not do anything

For being yourself

You are just a simple

Conscious being

This awareness of yourself

In every situation...

Knocks off

The piled up reactions

Which make a personality

You are just a person

A person is always a person

Who has appointments to keep...

Roles to play...

Scripts to follow...

It is very simple

And this is action

The personality

Is created by reactions

Whereas the person

Always acts

Oṁ Tat Sat

Books by Swami Dayananda Saraswati

Public Talk Series :

1. Living Intelligently
2. Successful Living
3. Need for Cognitive Change
4. Discovering Love
5. The Value of Values
6. Vedic View and Way of Life

Upaniṣad Series :

7. Muṇḍakopaniṣad
8. Kenopaniṣad

Prakaraṇa Series :

9. Tattvabodhaḥ

Text Translation Series :

10. Śrīmad Bhagavad Gītā
    (Text with roman transliteration and English translation)
11. Śrī Rudram
    (Text in Sanskrit with transliteration, word-to-word and verse meaning along with an elaborate commentary in English)

Stotra Series :

12. Dīpārādhanā
13. Prayer Guide
    (With explanations of several Mantras, Stotras, Kirtans and Religious Festivals)

Moments with Oneself Series :

14. Freedom from Helplessness
15. Living versus Getting On
16. Insights
17. Action and Reaction
18. Fundamental Problem
19. Problem is You, Solution is You
20. Purpose of Prayer
21. Vedanta 24x7
22. Freedom
23. Crisis Management
24. Surrender and Freedom
25. The Need for Personal Reorganisation
26. Freedom in Relationship
27. Stress-free Living
28. Om Namo Bhagavate Vāsudevāya
29. Yoga of Objectivity
30. Īśvara in One's Life

Bhagavad Gītā

31. Bhagavad Gītā Home Study Course (Hardbound - 9 Volumes)

Meditation Series :

32. Morning Meditation Prayers
33. What is Meditation?

Essays :

34. Do all Religions have the same goal?
35. Conversion is Violence
36. Gurupūrṇimā
37. Dānam
38. Japa
39. Can We?
40. Moments with Krishna
41. Teaching Tradition of Advaita Vedanta
42. Compositions of Swami Dayananda Saraswati

Exploring Vedanta Series : (*vākyavicāra*)

43. śraddhā bhakti dhyāna yogād avaihi ātmānaṁ ced vijānīyāt

Books translated in other languages and in English based on Swami Dayananda Saraswati's Original Exposition

Tamil

44. Veeduthorum Gitopadesam (9 Volumes)
    (Bhagavad Gītā Home Study Course)
45. Dānam

Kannada

46. Mane maneyalli Adhyayana (7 Volumes)
    (Bhagavad Gītā Home Study Course)
47. Vedanta Pravesike

Malayalam

48. Muṇḍakopaniṣad

Telugu

49. Kenopaniṣad

Hindi

50. Ghar baithe Gītā Vivechan (Vol 1)
    (Bhagavad Gītā Home Study Course)
51. Antardṛṣṭi (Insights)
52. Vedanta 24X7
53. Kriya aur Pratikriya (Action and Reaction)

Marathi

54. Gruhe Gītā Adhyayan (Vol 1 available)
    (Bhagavad Gītā Home Study Course)

English

55. The Jungian Myth and Advaita Vedanta
56. The Vedantic Self and the Jungian Psyche
57. Salutations to Rudra
58. Without a Second

Biography (Hardbound Deluxe)

59. Swami Dayananda Saraswati
Contributions & Writings
(Smt. Sheela Balaji)

Biography (Hardbound Regular)

60. Swami Dayananda Saraswati
Contributions & Writings
(Smt. Sheela Balaji)

Also available at :

ARSHA VIDYA RESEARCH
AND PUBLICATION TRUST
32 / 4 Sir Desika Road
Mylapore Chennai 600 004
Telefax : 044 - 2499 7131
Email : avrandpt@gmail.com
Website : www.avrpt.com

ARSHA VIDYA GURUKULAM
Anaikatti P.O.
Coimbatore 641 108
Ph : 0422 - 2657001
Fax : 0422 - 2657002
Email : office@arshavidya.in
Website : www.arshavidya.in

ARSHA VIDYA GURUKULAM
P.O.Box 1059. Pennsylvania
PA 18353, USA
Ph : 001 -570 -992 -2339
Email : avp@epix.net
Website : www.arshavidya.org

SWAMI DAYANANDA ASHRAM
Purani Jhadi, P.B.No. 30
Rishikesh, Uttaranchal 249 201
Telefax : 0135 - 2430769
Email : ashrambookstore@yahoo.com
Website : www.dayananda.org

Other leading Book Stores:

Chennai:	**044**
Motilal Banarsidass	2498 2315
Giri Trading	2495 1966
Higginbothams	2851 3519
Pustak Bharati	2461 1345
Theosophical Publishing House	2446 6613 / 2491 1338
The Odessey	43910300
Bengaluru:	**080**
Gangarams	2558 1617 / 2558 1618
Sapna Book House	4011 4455 / 4045 5999
Strand Bookstall	2558 2222, 2558 0000
Vedanta Book House	2650 7590
Coimbatore:	**0422**
Guru Smruti	9486773793
Giri Trading	2541523
New Delhi:	**011**
Motilal Banarsidass	2385 8335 / 2385 1985
Trivandrum:	**0471**
Prabhus Bookhouse	2478397 / 2473496

Kozhikode:	**0495**
Ganga Bookhouse	6521262
Mumbai:	**022**
Chetana Bookhouse	2285 1243 / 2285 3412
Strand Bookstall	2266 1994 / 2266 1719/ 2261 4613
Giri Trading	2414 3140
Bardoli (Surat):	**0622**
Dr. Anil Patwardhan	220283
(BGHS course - Marathi)	0-9377715684
Mysore :	
Swamini Varadananda	0-9242890144
(BGHS course - Kannada)	0-8762464014